WRITING AND RESEARCH

A Manual for Police Officers

MALCOLM HIBBERD

Reports in the Police Foundation series are published as an information service. The analysis, arguments, conclusions and recommendations in this report are those of the author and not necessarily those of the Foundation.

British Library Cataloguing in Publication Data

Hibberd, Malcolm
Writing and research: a manual for police officers.
1. Research reports. Compilation
I. Title
001.4

ISBN 0-947692-21-5

Published by the Police Foundation
314/316 Vauxhall Bridge Road, London SW1V 1AA
Printed by Anthony Rowe Limited, Chippenham, Wiltshire.

CONTENTS

LIST OF FIGURES

FOREWORD

The pressures for results-based assessment and planning in the police service - in current shorthand, demonstrating value for money - have probably never been greater. While Circular 114/83 provides the most explicit statement of the need for better evaluation as a precondition for the most effective management of resources, the importance of assessment and monitoring is a recurring theme in government policy statements on the police. These pressures have led to an upsurge in interest in and demand for research by the police service. An increasing amount of that research is now being carried out within police forces themselves.

Although police forces are being asked to do more research and monitoring, research knowledge and skills within the service are in short supply. This book and its companion volumes are designed to provide a comprehensive guide to planning and carrying out research in the police service, and to its role in police management. Unlike conventional methodological texts, the books are aimed specifically at a police audience; they address police managerial concerns and use examples drawn from police work to illustrate research methods and problems. We hope they will become essential reading for any police officer who is asked to collect and evaluate information, whether for a small-scale survey of local users of police services, or for a more complex study of the effects of changes in, say, the patterns of shift work on police morale and police effectiveness.

The manuals are already proving their worth. They are used as a basis for Malcolm Hibberd's regular contributions to the Greater Manchester Police course on research skills, and the Research and Planning Carousel at the Police Staff College.

The Foundation would like to thank the Home Office for a grant towards the cost of writing and producing these manuals. If our readers have any comments or suggestions on their content, we would be very pleased to hear from them.

Mollie Weatheritt
Assistant Director, The Police Foundation

PREFACE

In one sense, this manual can be seen as the last in the series to which it belongs. If research in an organisation is to be useful, its conclusions must be presented to decision makers in an accurate, clear and accessible way. This is done by writing and presenting a research report, the culmination of a research project. This manual explains how the technicalities of research should be presented in such a report.

In another sense, this manual should be the first in the series. A consistent theme of the series is that good research depends on careful planning, particularly in the early stages, the thinking that goes on before anything is actually done. Of all the work involved in a project, this is the hardest: the research question or problem must be clearly set out, concepts and variables defined, and assumptions stated. This requires the researcher to think logically and clearly, and to identify and put right any faults or inconsistencies. Clear writing and careful attention to the meaning of words is essential to this, and underlying much of what is said in this manual is the idea that clear writing is the royal road to clear thinking.

Chapter One briefly explains why writing is important in research. Chapter Two presents a series of ten rules for good writing, to be applied in both presenting research findings, and clarifying the researcher's own thinking. Chapter Three explains the purposes of research reports, how they should be structured and set out for different audiences. The last two chapters describe the sections included in a research report, Chapter Four covering the essential sections, and Chapter Five discusses sections that are optional, or only needed in certain types of report.

Malcolm Hibberd
London, 1990.

If language is not correct, then what is said is not what is meant; if what is said is not what is meant, then what ought to be done remains undone.

Confucius, quoted in Gowers (1973)

CHAPTER ONE

WHY WRITING IS IMPORTANT

THE BENEFITS OF GOOD WRITING

Writing is a very valuable research skill, although its importance is underestimated, and often overlooked. Paying close attention to the way you write will benefit you in at least four ways, namely:

- getting your ideas clear,
- recording what happens,
- getting your report read,
- understanding other reports.

These benefits are discussed briefly below, and covered in more detail in the rest of the manual.

Getting your ideas clear

In Research and Evaluation: A Manual for Police Officers, great emphasis is placed on the careful definition of the research problem, and the associated concepts and variables.

Paying close attention to the precise meaning of your definitions will help to expose any weaknesses in your thinking. To achieve this, you must discipline yourself to write clearly. If what you write is vague, then the underlying thinking may also be vague - but you will not be able to tell, precisely because it is vaguely expressed. If the language is clear, however, you will be able to identify any weaknesses in the underlying thinking.

Clarifying the way you write will help you to clarify and refine the way you think. More detailed advice on doing this is given in Chapter Two.

Recording what happens

When you get to the end of a long and complex research project, it is easy to forget what has happened in the early stages. This will make it difficult to present an accurate report of the project. To overcome this problem, you should get into the habit of keeping a written record of everything that happens.

The best way to do this is to keep a loose-leaf research log, for your private use. In it you can record your definitions of key concepts, records of events, as well as copies of correspondence, *pro formas*, and any other relevant paperwork; you can even keep a record of your own private thoughts, feelings and frustrations! Having all this information to hand will help you greatly when you come to write up your research report.

Getting your report read

Police decision makers have vast quantities of paper to read. They may be hard pressed or even reluctant to read a research report.

To increase your chances of getting read and taken notice of, try to make reading your report a more attractive proposition. There are four ways of doing this:

- make it as short as possible, and if it has to be long, produce a *management summary*;
- present it attractively - if it looks professional, it is more likely to be taken seriously;
- write in a snappy style, with short sentences and no digressions;
- give it a clear structure, with a list of contents and accurate summaries to all sections.

More detailed advice on these points is given later in the manual.

Understanding other reports

The more critical you are of the way you write, the more sensitive you will be to the way other people write. This means that the better you write, the easier it will be for you to understand and evaluate other people's research reports. Attention to the use of words will help you develop a questioning mind and enable you to judge for yourself whether results mean what they appear to mean.

CHAPTER TWO

GOOD WRITING FOR RESEARCH

INTRODUCTION

Writing style is a matter of personal taste, and I am neither willing nor indeed qualified to pronounce on what is good writing, or to give advice on writing elegant prose. In research, however, writing has a job to do; this makes it possible to lay down criteria for good writing in this particular context.

Clarity and conciseness

Writing has two purposes in research: first, to communicate ideas to other people (and to some extent yourself), and second, to keep an accurate record of what happens. If this is to be done effectively and efficiently, writing must have two qualities: *clarity* and *conciseness*.

The more important of these is clarity. The meaning of what you write should be directly and clearly understood by the reader; there should be no ambiguity.

Conciseness can help to make things clear, although a longer sentence will sometimes be easier to understand than a short one. Try to use as few words as possible, as long as you can do so without loss of clarity.

How to use this chapter

This chapter presents ten rules for good research writing. Refer to them when you are editing what you have written. Read through what you have written, thinking about what you mean to say, and ask yourself whether any of the rules will help you to get the meaning across better.

The ten rules, which are listed in Figure 2.1 on page 5, and explained in the following pages, serve two general aims, which you should always have in mind when writing.

Always say what you mean. Your report presents your findings and ideas, and it should do so accurately. Tell it as it is, and don't hide anything - even if this means admitting you don't know the answers, or that you are unclear about something.

Always take account of your reader. Put yourself in the position of the person who has to read your report, and make it as easy - and even enjoyable - as possible.

1. KEEP SENTENCES SHORT

2. ENSURE THAT EVERY WORD SERVES A PURPOSE

3. AVOID JARGON

4. AVOID CLICHES

5. USE PLAIN WORDS

6. USE THE CORRECT WORD

7. WRITE IN PARAGRAPHS

8. WRITE IN SECTIONS

9. MAKE LISTS

10. USE DIAGRAMS

Figure 2.1 Ten rules for good writing in research.

RULE ONE

KEEP YOUR SENTENCES SHORT

Why?

A sentence is a string of words that conveys a meaning. The same meaning can be conveyed by different sentences, some short, others long. It is usually best to opt for a short sentence.

What you write in a report will be either a series of facts or a reasoned argument. Whichever it is, the meaning that you want to communicate will follow a series of steps. To understand what you have written, the reader has to follow the same steps. The shorter the steps, the easier they will be to follow.

Short sentences will help to give you a wider readership. People will be more likely to read a document right through if you don't tire them out with long, rambling sentences.

How?

There are two ways to keep sentences short.

First, you can increase the number of sentences. If you have written a long sentence to express a long argument, it is usually possible to break the argument up into a series of steps. Each step can then be expressed as a short sentence. This will not reduce the overall length, but it will make the argument easier to follow.

Second, you can reduce the number of words. Most of us use a lot of words we don't actually need, so cutting them out can be quite easy. Try not to repeat yourself - if something is said clearly, then it need only be said once. Avoid *padding* in your report. Padding adds words to a sentence without adding any meaning. A few people may be impressed by sheer weight of words, but most will be put off by it. Rule Two below will help you to cut out unnecessary words.

An example

Here is an example of what can be achieved by cutting out words. (Version A is taken from a police research report.)

Version A - 43 words

The foregoing description of resources, demands and operational deployment at Eastwood subdivision are sufficient in themselves to indicate that the amount of time available to officers attached to the reliefs, to engage in formal and organised contact with the public, is severely limited.

Version B - 17 words

In conclusion, relief officers at Eastwood have little time for formal and organised contact with the public.

Version A is a sentence to grapple with. You read it a few times and then stop to wonder what it means. Version B simply says what it means in a direct and simple way, without going round the houses. Yet the meaning is exactly the same.

The most striking reduction comes from changing *The foregoing description of resources, demands and operational deployment ... are sufficient in themselves to indicate...* to *In conclusion...* At first sight these two passages do not appear to say the same. But consider that the reader has just read the description of resources and so on, so all you need to say is what follows from it - that is, the conclusion.

This sort of reduction would reduce a twenty page document to seven or eight pages.

RULE TWO

ENSURE THAT EVERY WORD SERVES A PURPOSE

Why?

Sentences convey meaning through words. Every word should contribute something to the meaning of its sentence. A word should never be redundant - each one should have a job to do.

In version A of the example above, the words *Eastwood police subdivision* are used. The words are from a police report, written for a police audience. In that context, all you need to do is refer to the area: the reader already knows that it is a police subdivision, so the words *police subdivision* serve no purpose. They are mere padding, wasting your space and the reader's time.

Ensuring that every word serves a purpose is the best way to keep sentences short.

How?

Writing a report isn't simply a matter of putting your thoughts on paper, getting it typed up and then presenting it. You produce a rough draft, edit it, and go through a succession of drafts, each one improving on the last, up to the final version.

It is when you are editing that you should check that every word serves a purpose. If you have written sentences with unnecessary words, then rewrite them. Rewriting can be simple or complex. Simple rewriting merely involves cutting out redundant words; complex rewriting involves reorganising the sentence.

Dropping redundant words. Once you get used to the idea that every word must serve a purpose, you will find that many words can be simply dropped from a sentence because they have no job to do.

In the following sentence, the underlined words serve no purpose, and can be dropped:

> *Basically, anti-shoplifting patrols are the top priority for the police in the town centre.*

These words are redundant for different reasons.

Basically. This is an overused word. It is easy to slip it into your writing because it has a conversational flavour, but it rarely adds any meaning. It merely announces that you are about to say something. But no announcement is needed - just say what you have to say.

Anti. It hardly needs saying that a police operation concerned with shoplifting will be anti-shoplifting. If you just say *shoplifting patrols* in this context, no one will think that the police are doing the shoplifting.

Top. The phrase *top priority* is *tautological* - it repeats itself. It's rather like saying *round circle.* A priority is defined as the most important thing - it is top by definition. So *top* is not needed. (In certain contexts it may be necessary to say *top priority*, or *first priority*. This would be where you have a list of ordered priorities - first, second, third, and so on.)

Reorganising the sentence. This needs a little more imagination. You will often find that a word serves no purpose, but that simply dropping it would make a nonsense of the sentence.

In version A of the example on page 7, the phrase *officers attached to the reliefs* is used. The only essential words here are *officers* and *reliefs*, but if we just drop the others, we are left with *officers reliefs*, which doesn't make much sense. All we have to do, however, is turn the words round to get *relief officers*, which is all that was meant. Such a simple reorganisation will often allow you to remove unnecessary words.

RULE THREE

AVOID JARGON

Why?

Jargon words and phrases are technical terms. If there is a chance that your readers will not understand the jargon, then try to avoid using it.

Jargon stands in the way of the idea you are trying to convey. If the reader doesn't know what a word means, then the idea will be unclear.

How?

Jargon is not always easy to root out. In getting rid of it, you often end up using extra words. But keeping the meaning clear is the most important thing. So if a single word of jargon can be replaced by a phrase of six simple words, the phrase will usually be better.

In the following example, the meaning is hidden away behind a statistical term:

The modal response to this question was 'strongly agree'.

The same meaning is conveyed by:

The most frequent response to this question was 'strongly agree'.

One of the problems with using jargon is that you often don't realise that you are using it. If you know a subject, you can easily forget that other people don't know the technical terms. It is a good idea to get someone who is not an expert in your field to look through what you have written and pick out words which they don't understand.

You may also find that a jargon word or phrase also serves no purpose. If a sentence begins:

Linear regression analysis shows that...

you should ask yourself whether the reader needs to know this. If it is a police audience, they will probably neither know nor care what it means. They will just want to know what the analysis shows. The technical details should be available - perhaps in an appendix, or a separate volume - but they needn't be read as a matter of course.

Exceptions

It isn't always necessary to avoid jargon; neither is it always possible.

Jargon can be appropriate. Like any other specialists, the police have their own jargon. Phrases like *relief officers*, *late turn* or *quick changeover* are widely understood by the police, so there is no harm in using them if you are writing for a police audience.

Sometimes a technical term may be needed repeatedly. In that case, it is probably better to use the jargon word rather than have the same six word alternative cropping up again and again.

There may be no simple alternative to using jargon. The term *statistical significance* cannot be replaced by a simple phrase; neither can *performance indicator*, or *semi-structured interview*.

If you cannot avoid jargon, and there is a chance that the audience will not know the meaning of a word or phrase, then you must define it carefully the first time you use it. If you use a number of technical terms, it is a good idea to define them all in an appendix or glossary.

RULE FOUR

AVOID CLICHES

Why?

A cliche is an overused word or phrase. Sometimes it has been used so much that it has lost all meaning and become mere padding.

Cliches give a familiar, conversational tone to writing. Because they are overused, they don't encourage the reader to pay close attention to the meaning of the words. Your writing must capture the reader's attention, and to do this it must be fresh. Cliches cannot be fresh because they are tired out from overuse.

Here is a sentence with two very tired cliches underlined:

> *At the end of the day, the research team recommends that the committee take on board the following proposals.*

The first can be dropped altogether; the second can be replaced by the word *adopt*. The result is somehow crisper than the original:

> *The research team recommends that the committee adopt the following proposals.*

The new sentence is eight words shorter and conveys the meaning more clearly and directly.

How?

It is not easy to avoid cliches. You must first of all be able to identify them, and this is difficult because they are so very familiar. There are two tips which may help you, however.

First, look at some examples of cliches. A few are given below, and more can be found in some of the books suggested at the end of this chapter. Look out for examples in what you read and, more importantly, in what you write. This will give you a feel for the sort of words and phrases that are overused.

Second, if you follow the other rules given here (especially the Rule Two), you will become more sensitive to the way we use words. This will make it easier for you to detect cliches.

Examples

Here are a few of the hundreds of examples of cliches could be given; look out for these - and others - in reports and conversation; try to think of how they can be avoided.

at the end of the day

at this moment in time (meaning now)

in this day and age

when all's said and done

over the top

take on board

in the dark (meaning ignorant)

coming home to roost

the beginning of the end

leave no stone unturned

RULE FIVE

USE PLAIN WORDS

Why?

Some people are impressed by a report that sends them scurrying to the dictionary, but most find this a bore.

Your job is to communicate the *meaning* of your research. You should not try to communicate how many long words you know. The most impressive thing you can do is to write clearly and simply.

Common words are preferable to unusual or rarely used words. *Lacuna* is a nice word, but in a research report it is better to use *gap*.

Common words also tend to be shorter. Shorter words are usually better, even if the reader knows what the longer word means. So common words are quicker to read and understand. Take the following sentence, typical of the language used in research reports:

There is a requirement for a new form to be utilised.

By changing two words we get a plainer sentence:

There is a need for a new form to be used.

(With only a little imagination we can change it to *a new form is needed*, which is better still.)

How?

We usually know when we are using a word which other people may not understand, and it is usually easy to find an alternative. Technical terms are special case, as there may not be a simple alternative (see Rule Three).

The use of long but familiar words is more subtle. Writers often feel that short words don't carry as much weight as long words. This may be true, but short words carry their meaning more efficiently, and that is more important.

When you are editing, look out for long words. When you find one, ask yourself if there is a shorter, more common alternative. A thesaurus and dictionary will help. It is also a good idea to get someone else to read through your drafts to check for long and unusual words.

RULE SIX

USE THE RIGHT WORD

Why?

To do research you have to think. You use words to think, and the product of your thinking is written down in a report.

Words are your tools. Each one has a job to do. Just as a carpenter takes care to select the right chisel for a job, so you should take care to select the right word.

If you don't choose the right word, the job will not be done properly. If you choose the wrong word, you will convey the wrong idea. If you choose a vague word, you will convey a vague idea.

How?

Using the right word is the hardest thing of all to do, as there are so many available. But choosing the right word gets easier if you constantly remind yourself that each word in a sentence has a job to do. Ask yourself two questions:

- what is the job to be done? (that is, what meaning do I want to convey?)

- does the word I have chosen do that job?

You may well find that your ideas are vague. Vague ideas can only be expressed in vague language, and research reports must not be vague. If you find that it is your thoughts, and not just your words, that are vague, you should rethink your ideas to make them more precise.

Usually, however, you will have a clear idea of what you want to say, but the words you have chosen don't do the job properly. In that case, you should spend more time trying to choose the right words.

A dictionary and a thesaurus may be useful for this. But you will often be able to think of the word for yourself, especially if you remember to aim for the simple word.

Examples

Take particular care when you are reporting findings and conclusions. Don't say something is *proven* if it is only *indicated*, and don't say it is *indicated* if it is only *suggested*.

If you have carried out a statistical test, you may find that a result is *significant*; if you haven't done a statistical test, the result may be *interesting* or *important*, but it cannot be *significant* (see <u>Basic Statistics: A Manual for Police Officers</u>). If an event *implies* a conclusion, you can *infer* the conclusion from the event, but not the other way round.

Many more examples of how to use words properly are given in some of the books listed at the end of this chapter.

RULE SEVEN

WRITE IN PARAGRAPHS

Why?

A sentence is a collection of words used to express an idea. A paragraph is a collection of sentences with the same purpose (although a paragraph may only have one sentence).

Paragraphs have a theme. They enable you to break the argument into chunks. A change of paragraph tells the reader that one theme has been dealt with and that a new, possibly related theme is about to begin. By breaking your argument into paragraphs, you make it easier for the reader to understand.

How?

Paragraphs should be kept short. Within a paragraph, each sentence should follow on directly from the previous one. If it doesn't, you should probably begin a new paragraph.

If the theme changes, or the line of argument shifts, then you should definitely begin a new paragraph.

RULE EIGHT

WRITE IN SECTIONS

Why?

It is very important for a research report to be clearly structured and divided into sections. The appropriate sections for a research report are discussed in Chapters Four and Five.

Different types of information should appear in different sections, and there are conventions for what should go where. This makes reports easier to understand: if the reader only wants to know a certain piece of information, then properly headed sections indicate where that information is to be found.

It also helps the reader to read the whole report. A well structured report shows clearly where it has been, and where it is going.

How?

Paragraphs are to sections as sentences are to paragraphs. Within a section, each paragraph should follow on from the previous one, picking up ideas and taking them further.

Each paragraph should *belong* under its section heading. When you have drafted your report, read each section and ask yourself if every paragraph is appropriate to that section. For example, you should not mention your *findings* in the *introduction*; this will confuse and annoy the reader.

The purpose of sections is to enable the reader to digest the report quickly. The reader should know where to look for a particular piece of information. You should make the reader feel that the report is well organised, otherwise it will look unprofessional and less authoritative.

Each section should be given a clear heading. Make sure that you label section headings consistently. Don't start with an **INTRODUCTION** and end with **Conclusions**. If there are subsections within sections, you should use a different form of heading - underlined capitals for section headings, perhaps, and underlined lower case letters for subsection headings.

RULE NINE

MAKE LISTS

Why?

When you are writing up research you will often have a series of points to make. Avoid listing your points *within* a sentence: it is better to list things *vertically*, and to indent the list. This will enable the reader to get an impression of the whole list at one glance.

How?

The following sentence from a research report is clearly written and includes all the relevant facts:

> *The project used diaries, observation techniques and semi-structured interviews to investigate the work of the community constable.*

However, it would be better presented like this:

> *The following methods were used to investigate the work of the community constable:*
>
> - *diaries,*
> - *observation techniques,*
> - *semi-structured interviews.*

Although this takes up more space, it makes the information more accessible, and so does a better job.

Research reports often include series of points, each explained in a separate paragraph. In such cases you should announce what you are going to say using a vertical, indented list. Then you should say it, paragraph by paragraph, with each paragraph under the appropriate heading from the list. Here is an example:

There are three reasons why this is the best option:

> *1. Effect on crime*
> *2. Effect on public relations*
> *3. Cost*

1. <u>Effect on crime</u>. The research shows that...

This helps enormously: the reader knows what is coming, and is therefore more receptive to each successive point.

RULE TEN

USE DIAGRAMS

Why?

A picture has an immediate impact, and can convey an idea more quickly than words. Rather than list endless statistics, it is usually better to give a table or diagram, and then discuss its main features.

How?

The visual presentation of information is discussed in detail in <u>Basic Statistics: A Manual for Police Officers</u>.

Always make sure that your tables and diagrams are properly labelled. There should be an explanation of what the table or diagram shows, either immediately above or below the figure.

Tables and diagrams should also be numbered so that they can be easily referred to in the text, and you should make sure the text refers to the correct ones. Labelling figures is one of the last jobs in editing. If you have a lot, and decide to put in a new one near the beginning, this will throw out all the subsequent numbers. If this happens, make sure the adjustments are made to the titles and the text, otherwise the report will not only be confusing, it will also look amateurish.

Finally, don't use diagrams indiscriminately, only when they help to illustrate a point in the text. Other figures can be put in an appendix, but only essential ones should appear in the text.

RECOMMENDED BOOKS

All writers will need to refer to a good dictionary and thesaurus from time to time. Apart from these, there are many useful books on writing style and use of English. These will offer additional advice, and amplify some of the points made in this chapter. The following standard works are useful; the second on the list is essential reading.

The Economist. *Pocket Style Book.* The Economist. 1986

Gowers, Sir E. *The Complete Plain Words.* Penguin Books. 1973

Fowler, H.W. *Modern English Usage.* Oxford University Press. 2nd edition, revised by Sir Ernest Gowers, 1968.

Partridge, E. *Usage and Abusage.* Penguin Books. 1973.

CHAPTER THREE

WRITING A RESEARCH REPORT

Once the findings of a research project have emerged, they must be presented to the appropriate audience. Among other things, this brings everything to a neat conclusion, and ensures that the research is an open process.

THE FORM OF THE REPORT

Some form of written report should always be available for a research project, even if the results are to be presented orally; often, two separate reports will be needed, a full version and a management summary.

The appropriate form for a research report depends on two factors:

- the nature of the research - what it is about, and what the findings consist of;
- the likely audience - the recipient of the report, and any other people who may need or want to read it.

Research reports vary chiefly in the amount of detail they contain. The most detailed reports are written for an academic audience, such as those presented in fulfilment of degrees, or for publication in academic journals. Such reports are often technical, although they are not necessarily long.

The least detailed report is the *management summary*. This simply states that research has been done, and presents the main findings and recommendations. Management summaries are short, often no more than three or four pages, and very much practically oriented.

The sort of report most often required in police research lies between these two extremes, and probably comes closer to the management summary. However, bear in mind that decision makers may want to see more detailed evidence, so a more detailed document should be available on request, perhaps as an appendix to the main report.

THE STRUCTURE OF THE REPORT

A research report must always be carefully structured. This means two things:

- the material should be presented in logical order, without repetition;
- the material should be presented in distinct sections, each clearly labelled to indicate what sort of information it comprises.

A good structure makes a report easier to read, since the route through it is direct and well signposted. This is best achieved by following certain conventions in report writing - standard sections, always containing the same type of information. If you read a few published research reports, you will appreciate the value of careful structuring.

The different sections of a research report are discussed below. Some will be needed in all research reports, and these are discussed in Chapter Four; others are optional, or only required in some reports, and these are discussed in Chapter Five.

While you are writing a report, bear in mind that it won't be destroyed after it has been read: it will sit on a shelf, and may be referred to again. However humble, a report becomes a source of knowledge, available for others to use. You should therefore write it so that it can be understood by someone who knows nothing about the background to the research report. Careful structuring helps you to do this.

SIGNPOSTING THE REPORT

The research report may be long and complex, so you should help the reader to negotiate it. This means it should be well labelled and signposted, so that the reader doesn't have to waste time trying to find things.

There are four basic considerations here. Attention to these will not only make it easier for the reader to understand, it will also give the report a more professional appearance. They are:

- title page,
- table of contents,
- page numbers,
- paragraph numbers.

Title page

The first thing the reader encounters in a research report is the title page. This should contain three things.

First, it should give the title of the research report. This should be an accurate and succinct summary of the purpose of the research. For example:

MANPOWER INFORMATION SYSTEM ON G DIVISION - EVALUATION AND IMPLEMENTATION STUDY.

ANALYSIS OF THE PATTERN OF BURGLARY FIGURES IN XYZ SUBDIVISION FOR 1989-90.

PUBLIC EXPECTATIONS OF THE POLICE ON C DIVISION - RESULTS OF A SURVEY OF THE COMMUNITY.

The title should be prominent and eye-catching, preferably typed in block capitals, underlined, and positioned in the centre of the page.

Second, it should give the name(s) of the researcher(s) who carried out the project, along with their ranks, if appropriate. This should be typed toward the bottom of the page.

Third, accompanying the names of the researchers, it should state the organisation or department where the research was carried out. This will usually be a department within a police force.

Since the title page is often the front cover of the report, it is worth paying some attention to layout and design.

Table of contents

The table of contents tells the reader where different types of information are to be found. It lists the sections and subsections that constitute the report, and gives their page numbers.

The contents table should be carefully set out, with sections and subsections clearly differentiated. One way to do this is to underline section headings and indent subsection headings, as in the example in Figure 3.1 on page 25.

If there are tables or figures in the report, these should be listed on a separate contents page, giving the number, title and page number of each table or figure.

Page numbers

Page numbers help you and the reader to refer to material elsewhere in the report.

If the report is longer than about ten pages, the pages must be numbered. If it is shorter, you need not number the pages as long as the paragraphs are numbered (see next section).

Paragraph numbers

The *conclusions* and *recommendations* sections of a report often quote material from elsewhere in the report. It is useful for the reader to refer to this other material, and this is easier if the paragraphs are numbered.

Paragraphs are usually numbered within sections. In the example of the table of contents given on page 25, the Introduction is section 2 of the report. If the paragraphs were to be numbered, the first would be 2.1, the second 2.2, and so on.

The numbering of paragraphs should also reflect subsections.

In the same example, Methodology comprises subsections 3.1 and 3.2. The numbering of the paragraphs in these two subsections would go:

Subsection 3.1 - paras 3.1.1, 3.1.2, 3.1.3, etc

Subsection 3.2 - paras 3.2.1, 3.2.2, 3.2.3, etc.

Paragraph numbers should appear in the margin, to the left of the first line of the paragraph.

The numbering should be done when the report is edited. If the report contains cross-referencing, make sure the correct numbers are given.

Paragraph numbering is optional, but very helpful. If the report is to be discussed by a committee, then the paragraph numbering is essential, as it will enable the committee to discuss the report paragraph by paragraph.

SECTION	PAGE
1. Summary	1
2. Introduction	2
3. Methodology	6
3.1 Activity analysis	6
3.2 Opinion survey	7
4. Results	9
4.1 Activity analysis	9
4.2 Opinion survey	14
5. Discussion and Recommendations	18
6. Conclusions	23
Appendix A	
Coding frame for activity analysis	24
Appendix B	
Opinion survey schedule	26

Figure 3.1 Model for setting out a table of contents.

EDITING A RESEARCH REPORT

A well written, properly structured report cannot be produced at a single sitting, but will have to be edited. Editing is the process whereby you move from the first draft of a report to the final, typed document. It involves looking for errors, tightening up the structure, checking that what you have written is justifiable, and ensuring that it is internally consistent in content and style.

You will have to go through several stages of editing what you write to ensure that your report is fluent, readable and free from errors. For simplicity, this process can be summarised as early editing and late editing.

Early editing - pulling the report into shape

In the early stages of editing, you should concentrate on pulling the report into shape. Your first draft will probably have been produced by putting together bits of material from different sources, written at different times. This means that it will be rather fragmented and incoherent. The following tasks are involved at this stage:

- ensuring that there is a continuous thread running through what you have written, so that everything in the report serves the central theme;

- checking that all the material is in the correct sections, and that within the sections the paragraphs follow on from each other to produce a coherent argument (see Rules Seven and Eight, pages 15-16);

- drawing up the diagrams and tables to be included in the text, deciding where they are to go, and giving them provisional numbers to indicate where they are to go and in what order;

- critically examining how you have expressed yourself, checking that everything you have written is clear and unambiguous, and that it has been said concisely (although never sacrifice clarity for the sake of conciseness).

Late editing - checking and polishing

In the later stages of editing you are more concerned with making the report look professional. You should aim to produce a report in which nothing distracts the reader from what is actually being said. The following tasks are involved:

- ensuring that the terminology and definitions used are consistent: if you change halfway through, the reader will be confused;

- giving the tables and figures their final numbers, and ensuring they are in the right place;

- numbering the pages and paragraphs (where appropriate);

- doing any cross-referencing that needs to be done; the text of your report may include references to tables and figures, and to other parts of the report: cross-referencing involves checking that the pages, paragraphs, tables and figures referred to are the correct ones;

- if you have a list of references (see pages 44-47), checking that all citations appear as references, and *vice versa*;

- checking spelling, punctuation and grammar;

- checking for typographic errors in the final draft;

- checking for consistent use of capitals and underlining in section and subsection headings.

The ten rules on writing given in Chapter Two should be applied when you are editing a report. This is particularly important in the early editing, when you should continually ask yourself if you have *actually* said what you *intended* to say, and whether what you have said is *justifiable* on the basis of evidence or reasoned argument.

PUTTING THE SECTIONS IN ORDER

Chapters Four and Five describe the main sections that comprise a research report, both essential and optional. Along with the title page and table of contents, they should be arranged in the order set out below.

1. Title page
2. Table of contents
3. Acknowledgements
4. Summary
5. Introduction (and literature review)
6. Methodology
7. Results
8. Discussion
9. Conclusions
10. Recommendations
11. References
12. Appendices

GETTING RESEARCH PUBLISHED

In Chapter One of Research and Evaluation: A Manual for Police Officers, research is described as an *open* process. This ideal is most fully realised when a research report is published, and becomes available to the rest of the research community. This means that specialists (and sometimes laypersons) are able to read, comment on and make use of your findings.

Publication will not always be appropriate: many police reports have a limited audience, and will be of interest only to decision makers within a police force.

However, you may feel that your research makes a more general contribution to our knowledge and understanding of police work or related issues. If so, you should consider submitting a version of your report to a journal, or for presentation at a conference.

There are a number of journals in which police research is published. Some are listed in Chapter Five of Research and Evaluation: A Manual for Police Officers; you can find out about others in libraries, or from the references given in books and articles. It is worth looking at back numbers of these to see what sort of things get published. The journals and relevant societies also advertise conferences at which papers can be presented.

Journals apply rigorous standards in selecting reports for publication. They have to be carefully argued, and the conclusions must be valid and properly supported. What is said in a published report usually has to be backed up by reference to previous research, cited in a literature review in the introduction.

Journals also require authors to submit articles in a standard format; most have a *house style*, details of which are available from the publishers, whose address will appear in the journal.

Articles submitted for publication are often returned to the author with a request for certain amendments to be made, after which the article will be published. They will also ask for corrections to be made. If the house style has not been followed, this will delay publication.

Of course, police and other government employees have to get permission to publish research findings, but that is usually a formality, unless the findings are confidential or sensitive. In a climate that is increasingly receptive to research, police forces are often keen to see their officers' work get into print. Take advantage of this: as a researcher you have a duty to publish interesting findings, and you should always consider the possibility that your research will be of general interest.

CHAPTER FOUR

ESSENTIAL SECTIONS OF A RESEARCH REPORT

The vast majority of research reports should include seven sections, namely:

- summary,
- introduction,
- methodology,
- results,
- discussion,
- conclusion,
- recommendations.

This chapter describes the function and content of each of these sections.

SUMMARY

The summary is sometimes called the *abstract*. It is an overview of the entire report, no more than a page in length. Its purpose is to tell the reader what the report is about. If someone has to read through a pile of reports, some of which may not be relevant, it is useful to be able to make a quick decision about whether a report is likely to be relevant or not. The summary enables the reader to do this, by providing a potted version.

The summary should contain a sentence or two on each of the following:

- the context or background of the research;

- the aims of the research;

- how the research was done;

- the main findings;

- the recommendations made.

It should contain little or no detail; numbers should not be given unless they are crucial to the findings; there should certainly be no tables or diagrams.

The summary is often the most difficult section to write, as it must be very concise, as well as clear. It is a good idea to make the summary the last thing you write, when you will be in in the best position to see the project as a whole.

The summary should say nothing that does not appear elsewhere in the report: it must say what the report says, only more briefly.

INTRODUCTION

The introduction of a report sets the scene, putting the research in context, and providing background material.

The introduction should begin by covering the following points:

- the organisational context of the research, describing sponsor, researcher and recipient of the project;

- the purpose of the research;

- where and when the research was done.

It should then present the subject matter of the research. This will include discussion of some of the questions that were considered in the early stages of planning, when the problem and key concepts were defined. The main concepts should be described and defined, and any assumptions should be stated.

Finally, and most importantly, there should be a clear statement of the problem definition, and (where appropriate) any hypotheses that the research sets out to test.

There is usually no need for an involved, logical exploration of concepts in the introduction. However, if there were any major conceptual problems in developing the research ideas, these should be discussed: say what the difficulties were and how they were resolved. For example, if you are using concepts which are difficult to define (such as stress, or morale) some discussion of the definitional problems should be included in the introduction.

The introduction should be at least two pages long, and may be more, depending on how complex the project is. It must contain enough material to enable the reader to understand what the research is all about, why it was carried out, and what questions it attempted to answer.

If a report is intended for an academic audience the introduction should include a *literature review*; this is discussed as an optional section on page 44.

METHODOLOGY

If the purpose of the Introduction is to explain why the research was carried out, the purpose of this section is to describe *how* it was carried out.

In a report written for an academic audience, the methodology section must be very detailed. However, most reports produced in the police service require less detail.

Three types of information are needed in the methodology section, namely:

- design,
- measures,
- sampling.

Design

The design should be described in a couple of paragraphs to show the strategy that was used to answer the question. For example, you should say whether it was a *before-and-after* design, or *cross-sectional*. If any controls were used, they should be described.

Under design you should also describe your main sources of information, for example whether a survey was carried out, or whether data were collected from existing records.

Measures

In describing the measures you should give *operational definitions* of the variables, and say which were dependent and independent, where appropriate.

If there are many variables, for example where a questionnaire is used, it is best to list only the key variables, and to describe the rest under a series of headings, such as:

- *standard demographic variables,*
- *experiences of crime,*
- *contact with the police.*

The instruments used in collecting the data (the questionnaires themselves, for instance) should *not* be included here, as this would interrupt the flow of the report. If needs be, they should go in an *appendix* (see pages 48-49). This also applies to *pro formas*, coding sheets, and so on.

Sampling

Finally, under sampling you should describe the *entities* you have looked at in your research.

For example, the entities may have been people, in which case you should say what sort of people, how many took part, how they were selected, whether any refused to take part, and so on.

Alternatively, the entities may have been areas, such as subdivisions, in which case you should say where they were, what area they covered, whether they were selected, and if so how, and so on.

Any specific sampling procedures used should be briefly described using standard terminology, such as *simple random sampling*, or *random sampling stratified by rank*. The mechanics of the sampling should not be described here. If needed, these details should go in an *appendix* (see pages 48-49).

RESULTS

This section presents the material on which the answers to the research question are based. What is needed here is a bald statement of the simple facts uncovered by the research.

Avoid any *interpretation* of the results in this section: the actual answering of the question should go in the discussion. The results section should merely contain the evidence on which the answer is based.

Four types of information should appear in the results section, although they will not always be needed. They are:

- tables of summary data,
- graphical representations of data,
- brief verbal statements of findings,
- details of inferential statistics.

Tables of summary data

Summary data are the result of the aggregation of raw data (see Basic Statistics: A Manual for Police Officers). Raw data should never appear in the results section. If they are needed, they should go in an *appendix* (see pages 47-50).

The tables in this section will contain *descriptive statistics*, usually frequencies, percentage frequencies and means; there may also be contingency tables. The descriptive statistics may be broken down by key variables, presenting results separately for different groups of people (or places, or events, and so on).

Tables communicate results most effectively if:

- they are kept simple including vital information only - anything else should go into an appendix;

- they are properly labelled, with headings for rows and columns, stating whether the figures are percentages, frequencies, and so on;

- the table itself is clearly and accurately labelled, with a single clear sentence for a title.

Tables should also be numbered, so that you can refer to them in the text of your report. The usual way is to give each table two digits, the first representing the chapter or section in which it appears, the second representing its number within the section. For example, *Table 3.5* would be the fifth table in section three, while *Table 5.1* would be the first in section five.

When you edit the report make sure that the text refers to the correct table. Also, tables should only be given if the results shown in them are discussed in the report.

Graphical representations of data

Results can be communicated very effectively by diagrams, which give the reader a more immediate impression than numbers alone. If you have an important finding to emphasise, present it in graphical form, as well as giving the results in a table.

The main types of graphical representation are:

- histograms,

- bar charts,

- pie charts,

- graphs,

- scatterplots.

They are discussed in Chapter Three of Basic Statistics: A Manual for Police Officers. Which you use will depend on the type of data you are dealing with.

As with tables, diagrams should be clear, as simple as possible, properly labelled, and given a title and a number. The numbering of diagrams follows the same principle as the numbering of tables. They are usually referred to as *Figure 1.1*, *Figure 1.2*, and so on. The numbers for tables and figures should run in separate sequences, so that you can have both a *Figure 3.2* and a *Table 3.2*.

Be sparing in your use of graphs. They tend to make a report *look* impressive and scientific, but you should not include them unless they are directly relevant to the research.

Brief verbal statements of findings

All findings should be presented verbally as well as in a table or diagram. Many findings would not be effectively presented in a table at all, for example:

> *Out of the 16 neighbourhood watch schemes on the division, 12 (75%) were set up at the request of the public.*
>
> *768 households were covered by the 16 schemes, giving a mean of 48 households per scheme.*
>
> *The largest scheme contained 113 households, while the smallest covered 19.*

Although these findings are numerical, they are best presented as short, snappy statements.

Even where a table (or figure) is provided, findings should also be described in words, with reference to the relevant table:

> *As can be seen from the frequency distribution in Table 3.10, the majority (58%) thought that the new shift system was a good idea; however, a substantial minority (31%) thought it was a bad idea, the rest (11%) being undecided.*

Here the writer has used phrases such as *substantial minority*, which give a good general impression of the findings; since these phrases are not precisely defined (when does a *minority* become *substantial*?) they are backed up by the figures.

Verbal statements of findings must be accurate, clear and concise.

Details of inferential statistics

If you have carried out any statistical tests, the details should be recorded alongside the findings which they apply to.

Don't include everything. For example, you need not quote formulae, nor do you need to include the *null and alternative hypotheses* (although they should be recorded in the research log for reference).

The details you must include are:

- the type of test or technique used,
- what figures the test was applied to,
- the value of the test statistic,
- the degrees of freedom,
- whether the test was one-tailed or two-tailed,
- the significance level.

This may seem a lot, but it can usually be summarised in a short sentence, such as:

> *Student's t test on difference between means, $t = 4.27$ with 18 d.f., one-tailed test, $p<0.001$.*

Sometimes there may be a table of findings, some of which are not significant, and the others being significant to different levels. When this is done, the usual practice is to indicate the significant findings by asterisks, and to include in the table a key to the appropriate significance levels, as shown in the following example:

Pearson Product Moment Correlation Coefficients, significance tested with t test, two-tailed, 28 degrees of freedom.

* : *0.05*
** : *0.01*
*** : *0.001*

Presenting extensive findings

In most cases, the statements of the findings should go into the results section, and the interpretation of them should go into the discussion.

This is not always best practice, however. If you have carried out a questionnaire survey, for example, there will be a lot of relevant findings to present. In that case it may be better to integrate the presentation and interpretation of the findings, and have a combined section called *Results and Discussion.* In this section you would discuss each finding before presenting the next one.

If you do this, the section should be broken down into clearly headed subsections, listed in the table of contents.

DISCUSSION

The results section presents a picture of *how* things have turned out in the research. The discussion section attempts to explain *why* things have turned out that way.

The depth of this explanation depends on the scope of the original research question. Some questions can be answered simply, others require more involved discussion, and even then may not be answered with any certainty.

In most cases, a lot of thought will need to go into the discussion. However, if the research has been properly planned along the lines laid down in Chapter Two of Research and Evaluation: A Manual for Police Officers, most of the thinking will already have been done: you should have anticipated the different ways the results could have turned out. While the actual results may surprise you, you should at least have considered the alternatives, and what they all mean in relation to your question.

Having asked the question in the introduction and looked at the facts in the results, in the discussion you decide what the facts say. This will mean doing the following things.

Relating the findings back to the questions.

In the simplest case this means providing the facts and figures required as direct answers to the question.

In more complex examples it means deciding whether a series of hypotheses has been supported or not, and coming to a balanced answer to a central question, such as whether a new scheme works or not.

The end product of this is your account of the findings.

Discussing alternative accounts of the findings.

Before you can account for the findings, you must consider alternative accounts. Your discussion should describe the alternative accounts and say why you chose one and rejected the others.

It may happen that there isn't enough evidence to decide, in which case you should explain that the question cannot yet be answered.

In simple projects where straightforward facts are required, you need not become involved in alternative accounts.

Drawing out the implications of your findings.

This means putting the findings into a practical context, saying what they mean for the audience. This usually means presenting them in such a way that they can be used by decision makers.

You should always say something about the *limitations* of the research: if you are in two minds about what you say, this should be clear from the discussion. A decision maker needs to know whether research evidence is clear or equivocal. Remember that research is one of the decision maker's tools, and the precision of the tool needs to be known if it is to be used profitably.

If your research is to be open, you should explain clearly how the conclusions were reached. That explanation should go into the discussion.

Everything you say in the discussion should be supported by at least one of the following:

- evidence from the research itself;
- evidence from elsewhere (usually other research);
- reasoned, logical argument.

You should not only show how the conclusions were reached, but also what sort of evidence they depend on.

CONCLUSIONS

The conclusions are a brief statement of what the research found. Research is about using the environment to learn. The conclusions should state what has been learned.

You should never conclude something unless it:

- follows from the results, and
- has been discussed in the discussion section.

The conclusions should follow on as a sort of summary section to the discussion. How long they should be will obviously depend on how involved the findings are - they can be as short as a single sentence. If the conclusions are longer, it is best to present them as a series of numbered sentences, possibly divided into subsections.

RECOMMENDATIONS

The final section of your report should state the practical applications of your findings. It is your view, as researcher, of what should be done.

The final decision may well be someone else's. But as the person who best understands what the research has come up with, your opinions should be included.

Make sure the recommendations really do follow from the research. You may have other opinions derived from years of experience, but your report should tell what the *research* says.

You may prefer to make recommendations within the report. As practical points arise in the discussion section, it makes sense to state recommendations immediately, particularly if there are a lot of them. This is perfectly acceptable, but bear two things in mind:

- recommendations should stand out from the text so that the reader can recognise them for what they are;
- it is useful to have a final summary section of recommendations which have been made throughout the report, so that they are all available in the same place.

If there are a lot of recommendations, they should be numbered and organised in subsections.

IN CONCLUSION...

The seven basic sections of the research report should form a coherent whole. Each one has its own function, and they all work together for a common purpose - to communicate the research findings.

Each section describes a different aspect of the process by which questions are answered. Since they all describe the same process, the contents of each section should be interrelated. Taking the sections in reverse order, this means that:

You must not *recommend*
what has not been *concluded*.

You must not *conclude*
what has not been *discussed*.

You must not *discuss* something
that is not part of the *results*

The *results* must not contain anything
that does not arise from the *methodology*.

The *methodology* must not describe the methods
of answering any questions that are not
set out in the *introduction*.

The *summary* must not contain anything
that does not appear anywhere else in the report.

CHAPTER FIVE

OPTIONAL SECTIONS OF A RESEARCH REPORT

In addition to the seven sections which all reports should contain, there are four which are either optional, or required in certain forms of report only. They are:

- acknowledgements,
- literature review,
- references,
- appendices.

These sections can be safely omitted if you are pressed for time. They are only likely to be required if your report is being submitted in fulfilment of an educational qualification or for publication.

ACKNOWLEDGEMENTS

If anyone has helped you in any way in your research, it is courteous to thank them. This should be done in the acknowledgements section, which should appear on a page of its own, between the title page and the table of contents.

As well as people who may have helped you with their expertise or ideas, you should thank typists and anyone else who helped you to prepare the report. These people should be referred to by name.

You may also wish to thank people who cannot be mentioned by name, such as *all the people who gave up their time to fill in the questionnaire.*

LITERATURE REVIEW

Strictly speaking, this is not a section in its own right, but a part of the *introduction.*

Whenever possible in research, you should carry out a literature review as part of your research planning. However, even if you have done one, it is not always advisable to include it in the report, since they tend to make a report lengthy, and may put people off reading it.

There are two situations when a literature review will usually be required. The first is when your research is being submitted in fulfilment of some academic or other educational requirement. The second is when you are hoping to get the report published in an academic journal.

If you do include a literature review in the introduction to your report, any research which you mention should be given a citation - a reference to who did the research and when it was published. Citations can appear in one of two forms, either:

- *Ekblom and Heal (1982) found that...*

or

- *It has recently been argued (eg Baldwin and Kinsey, 1982; Reiner, 1985) that...*

Any references that are cited in this way should be listed in the references section, described next.

REFERENCES

If any mention is made of what anybody else has said in a research report, a reference should be given. This enables the reader to check that what the other person said has been correctly reported.

If there are only a few occasions when you mention other people's work, the references can be put in as footnotes. However, if there are more than about five, they should be listed alphabetically in a separate section, immediately following the recommendations.

In most reports on police research you are unlikely to need a references section. However, if you have included a literature review in the research (see page 44) you should list the references; also, if you intend to get your report published, references will be required.

When listed, references should be given in a standard form. This gives information on who wrote the report, what the title is, who published it, and when it was published.

There are four types of publication that you are likely to come across, and they vary slightly in the way they should be presented. They are:

- books,
- articles in edited books,
- journal articles,
- reports produced by police forces and other organisations.

The standard way of presenting each one is explained below.

Books

The information needed for referencing a book is as follows, in the order in which it should be presented:

- name(s) of author(s) or editor(s),
- year of publication,
- title of book (this should be underlined),
- place of publication,
- name of publisher.

This information is presented as follows:

Bottomley, K. and Coleman, C. 1983 Understanding crime rates. Farnborough: Gower.

Articles in edited books

Here you will present the information for the *book* (minus the date), preceded by the following information on the *article*:

- name(s) of author(s) of article,
- year of publication,
- title of article (in inverted commas).

This is presented as follows:

Weatheritt, M. 1983 'Community policing: does it work and how do we know?', in: T. Bennett (ed.), The future of policing. Cambridge: University of Cambridge Institute of Criminology.

Journal articles

For journal articles you will need:

- name(s) of author(s) of the article,
- year of publication,
- title of journal (in inverted commas),
- name of journal (underlined),
- volume number (and issue number or month of issue, as appropriate),
- inclusive page numbers of article.

This is presented as follows:

Hough, M. 1980 'Managing with less technology.' British Journal of Criminology, 20, 344-57.

Reports produced by police forces and other organisations

For unpublished reports such as this, you will need:

- name(s) of author(s),
- year of publication,
- title of report (underlined),
- place of production (if known),
- name of organisation (and department, if appropriate).

This is presented as in the following example:

Butler, A.J.P. and Tharme, K. 1982 Social survey: Chelmsley Wood subdivision. Birmingham: Management Services Department, West Midlands Police.

The references section should only include references that are cited in the text, and every source that is cited should be included in the references.

The references should be presented in alphabetical order by author (or first named author if there are more than one).

APPENDICES

Research reports should be as short as possible; if they are long, people will be discouraged from reading them.

To keep reports short you must include only material that is of direct relevance to what you are saying. This may mean that you have to exclude material that you feel should be available to the reader for reference purposes.

The best way round this problem is to include the information in an appendix at the end of the report.

Of course, a weighty appendix will still make the report look bigger. But if you are worried about the effect this might have on your readership, you can produce a limited number of appendices as a separate volume, which can be made available to those who express an interest.

There are three types of information that are usually put into appendices, namely:

- methodological detail,
- findings that are of indirect relevance, or only of interest,
- sundry information.

Methodological detail

Included here is information that is not necessary for the report to be understood, but which is needed if the reader wants to check that the research has been properly done.

For example, if the research involved sampling in any way, the exact procedure used to draw the sample should be fully described in an appendix.

If your research involved classifying or coding material (such as in an *activity analysis*), you should include an appendix that contains the definitions of the categories, how they were devised, and any information you have on their *reliability*.

Technical information should not go in the main body of a report but in an appendix. This is because, unless your audience is highly specialised, the readers are unlikely to be interested or even able to understand the details.

In deciding whether methodological details are needed in a report, you should imagine another researcher who wants to repeat, or *replicate* your research, to check your findings. To do this, the other researcher would need to carry the research out exactly as you have done (or as near as possible). You should therefore include such detail as would make this possible.

Consequently, *pro formas* (including questionnaires) and other printed material (including letters asking subjects to cooperate) should appear in the appendix. Even if you don't actually include them, you should make them available on request, and point this out in the methodology section of the report.

Other findings

Most research generates more material than is strictly required for answering the question. However, only directly relevant findings should be reported in the body of the report. Consequently, you are likely to end up with indirectly relevant information, or information that could simply be interesting, which you feel is worth providing for your audience. Such material may be included in an appendix.

An example of such indirect but important information might arise in a survey of PCs' opinions. Opinions are affected by a wide range of variables, such as age, sex, length of service and so on. An informed reader may want to check that the opinions you describe are based on a representative sample of PCs, or whether the sample was biased in any way. To make it possible for such checks to be made, you should include a breakdown of your sample by age, sex, length of service and so on, in an appendix.

Any other findings that look interesting, or which may help other people in their research, can be put in an appendix.

Sundry information

There may well be other odds and ends that should be included for reference, but which would clutter up the main report. These too can be put in an appendix, and referred to in the text.

For example, you may be writing a report on neighbourhood watch. Such schemes tend to accrue various bits of official paper, such as newsletters, or letters from the Chief Constable inviting people to attend a meeting. Such material may be interesting to readers, particularly if they wish to compare practices with their own experiences.

You should not necessarily put all the extras into one appendix. If you have different types of material to include, you should put them in separate appendices, each one numbered or labelled in some way (usually Appendix A, Appendix B, and so on).

If your appendices are included in the main report, list them in the table of contents. If they appear in a separate volume, give that volume its own table of contents.

Finally, don't use appendices as a sort of dustbin for

information in a report. If they are used, appendices should have a purpose, and you should refer to the information contained in them at the appropriate points in the main report.